Whew! That Was Close-
I Almost Liked Her!...

By

Angela C. Williams

Whew! That Was Close-
I Almost Liked Her!...

By

Angela C. Williams

Whew! That was close!...I almost Liked her

Dedication

To Carlos Williams; my big brother
I Love Him

Just a Thought:

When men and women say things like; "You were a ho and you knew it;" I realize that I've been raised right and that I'm an educated, Christian woman in her right mind. I met Jesus at an early age. I married young, right out of college after joining a Christian sorority. Why would "I" want to be a ho? Sometimes I just imagine a reality show that is in actuality, a debate about motives, intentions and outcomes of relationship. See, I am unable to understand or constructively think that anyone would want to be treated like, or called a ho. I don't care if they are broke, ugly or if they had sex before they knew the other person's birthday. I will never understand how someone can judge their sexual experience with a person based on that person's sexual experience with a previous lover. Based on first-hand conversation or rumors. Neither makes sense to me. I will never understand the argument that someone wants to have sex without a commitment; without dating or without a focus to be married. The Word of God doesn't say you never say the righteous begging for bread because they will never lose their job; it's speaking of the kindness that should flow from that believer's around them. I can't take advantage of those blessings because you all forced me to sin. And God knows it. But the men who didn't choose me; say, "they walk the walk, but I just talk the talk" (regarding Christ). Basically the other woman had big titties and money and they told them no the first time they could have said yes sexually. That turned the guys on.

I know a lot of people who listen to nothing but Gospel music; and they don't know the first thing about having the heart of Christ. They think I'm the fake Christian. Everyone's entitled to their opinion. Just don't harass me with your opinion; please. I've never curled myself up into a ball after sex.

My daughter believes and says out loud that I'm a ho. She is very disrespectful. That's why I'm so surprised that she isn't more focused on school. She's disappointed in me and I'm disappointed in her and everyone else I've ever known. Everyone thinks I'm mean. I don't think you can get any meaner then leaving someone homeless with a kid and refusing to socialize with them so that they lose brain cells.

To all of the women who say to me," You need to wait." How long do I need to wait to have female friendship or steady educated conversation or "unlimited" income. There's something wrong with you all's brains. I'm not looking for a man. And I'm not gay. Not interested in having sex at all. I was never aggressive in that way.

The women are now saying just show her your penis. I didn't then nor do I know want see their penis. I wanted to go out either alone with my own money or with female friends. You made sure I only had enough money for the hotel and food.

The Blacks in this part of Maryland are trifling; whore-minded. I do not have hygiene issues and I've never sold sex. I'm not ghetto, I made a mistake at work once, but I am professional. The ghetto women have a dedicated man, regardless of the length of time before they became intimate. "perfect facial features" and a stable job. Even if their hair isn't real and their skin is all eaten up. Even if they curse at their little 3 year old. Even if they have lots of roaches.

See, those who set out to deceive their friends or potential or former mates, are trifling in any race, but all of the hell that Blacks already have to go through I life, why would we want to deceive each other by lying and saying "I'm working"; when I we're really off but hanging with someone else? While they are trying to figure out your lie; their not a ho, you're just an idiot. If you decide to tell them that you and they then realize that you are not that serious about them; that still makes YOU an idiot. That's why there are so many, hurt feeling and broken families in the Black community. People who do that, ruin it or those men who really are out there working hard, everyday. (The sad part is that there are men out here who believe that I would continue a an intimate relationship with a man who says he's off one day and I can't each him, all day).

I am aware that finances can keep a couple from spending a lot of time dating outside of free places such as the zoo or the museum but, love can be found in a lot of places and in a lot of ways. It truly just a matter of what each person wants. There are honest people who say what they want from the beginning and there are dishonest people who lie about what out of a relationship.

Do you ever wonder, why us ugly people don't just surrender to sharing a mate at an early age. Aren't we aware then that we are ugly, and later our riches won't change that. So why don't we just look for rich, ugly people? Or the physically challenged who wear a size A or B bra. Why don't they just share a mate from the beginning? (…you know I'm being sarcastic right)?

I've never really cared what other people believed about my sexual past but the spread of such incorrect information lead to sabotage of what I had left of a life. I was then forced to befriend guys who intimidated me into sex in "exciting places." Inappropriate but exciting. Now it's so that I can't even work. They're all insane. I've never had issues with hygiene and I do not struggle with the idea of not having sex. I don't really understand the "viewer's" obsession with me. It's baffling.

Unfortunately, there is a such thing as it being "too late to tell the truth". That's the way they all planned it. The Christians, the poor or whore-minded; the rich aristocrats or working professionals etc… I was Rio and they blamed it all on me; or they completely stopped talking to me and forced me to befriend old and new male persons only. These guys "knew" how "crazy" I was the first time they spoke with me right? So why even ask for my number? If I'm so crazy? Doing the same thing and getting the same results over and over is considered insanity. Well, I guess I could just sit and stare at the wall. Or I could go back to church and meet another guy who too thinks my breast are too small.

These aren't people I met at a club. Only a few of them I met actually on the street. When you live near-by for years or you go to school together or work together, you get familiar with one another.

You know, I never sit around saying, MAN, I slept with so many guys. But Hollywood felt the need to watch me and reveal my intimate partner count. Sadly, they lied about how, why and when things happened. The entertainment world told their lies about my life; the men in my life told their lies about their time with me. Now I tell the truth in my book. I suppose it will make life a little better to understand for my grandchildren. And my great grandchildren; even if no one else believes me.

In high school I was very popular and I was a good friend. I guess it was hard to ignore the fact that I was a girl but ultimately no guy wants a female jock for a life-mate. I mean gosh, I never wore tennis shoes to school.

Although staying in shape was important during college, and intramural basketball was a great way to do that, I neglected to join an organization that would allow me to take advantage of entry level positions in my field of Mass Communications. (This field should probably be renamed, Media Communications).

Everyone on the planet refuses to purchase any of my books. Well it's no secret that I married a man named Dustin; my daughter's father, but everything else has kind of been left up to your imagination. I have never been aggressive sexually with any man. No, I've never sold sex. Let me attempt to dispel the myths, rumors and lies:

Understand that in each case, I expected to continue talking and dating. I desired forever. Why wouldn't they? (Could it have been something they saw on TV, in a movie maybe)? Maybe my personality id a little too weird. It may come across as crazy to someone, too laid back. Unfortunately there's no medicine for silly. Unless I say I stopped talking to them, I never stopped calling until I realized they weren't gonna call me back. I just wonder what these guys relationships were like with the women that you readers and these men, don't consider ho's. (They didn't have sex until they had a ring). Yeah OK. And if that's the case, it's because they've been hurt by other guys and don't know them well enough. Being virtuous is not just, no having sex. It's your heart and mind-set toward people. How is it that I have no friends and can't get a ride from one Christian woman? I am not a ho.

I wasn't asked to the Prom because I'm not lite-skinned, I don't have big titties and, I wasn't having sex.

If I had two or three girlfriends, right now that were true friends and called me or contacted me by Facebook on a regular basis. If she and I went to concerts and movies and lunch and bowling every now and then, I would never think about how many men people SAY I slept with. I believe it was a Mary Kate and Ashley movie that stated," I don't need a psychiatrist, I need a friend". (My former best friend is a psychologist).

People think that if I'm crying it's because I'm single. The people who think that shouldn't be in a relationship with a man. I have a teenage daughter and I need to work. Period. Get over the fact that Hollywood is obsessed with me and leave me and my daughter alone when we are working. Stop the verbal harassment. I'm not a ho nor did I used to be. I'm being forced into a relationship with a man because this country refuses to let me work. They planned to make me lose my job because I was thriving without a man. I was very happy. They verbally harassed me to get me to leave and when it didn't work, they literally hit me. This country has forced my daughter into a relationship with a boy for financial support because they don't want me to be able to earn a living to support her. (I thank God for my grandbaby; he's a blessing).

Contrary to popular belief, and scenes from movies where my face is on the little girl, I have not been molested by anyone in my family or elsewhere.

And no, Ive never had sex with more than one person at a time.

I had my child within my marriage. I wasn't looking for a man. I'd joined a Christian sorority in college. I had a college degree. I had my own place, my own car and a good job. I was vigorously rebuilding my credit. I had a huge extended family that always had regular cook-outs at my mother's home and I was traveling, alone; using money from my own paycheck. (Rumor has it that I didn't shave the hair on my vagina, low enough).

Well, whatever it was; I'm still single.

In over 15- 20 years, I can't recall a lunch date with a female friend; (especially where they invited me). During the many years that I was left homeless, with and without my daughter, I was invited to lunch by a woman: to be told that, she, the mother of a man I'd grown-up with since Boys and Girls Club; that her son, was still single. I knew he didn't want me. We went on one date and he never called me again. (Contact him and ask him if I smelled. He's the one who had the twin brother who died in the fire.) She made me aware that she had breast cancer. I didn't know what to say. I was speechless. But sadly and more importantly, I was tearless. I was invited to lunch by an under- cover Federal Agent, former HS basketball team member; also, when I was homeless. She needed to tell me that my teen-aged daughter's boyfriend used to be in a gang. Then finally, after asking her; my soror agreed to take me to lunch. She made it a point to tell me that I'd pan-handled and the citation that I received may result in me going to jail. She told me to give my daughter her telephone number.

I'd seen the picture of several of the sorors from my chapter, at Arundel Mills; on Facebook. I guess they decided to invite me to an event this past year. We were all supposed to go to dinner. Only three people showed up not including myself. It's been exactly one year since then, I haven't heard from them. Oh, except for the one who wanted me to know that I might end up in jail.

If I don't contact them, I will probably never hear from them again. I'm 42. I wasn't pretending to be a Christian all of these years. I'm being forced to speed date, all of my life, without any female dates. You say every six months I had sex with a man. This happening from age 15 or 16 until age 42. Many are not mentioned, but if you count the men I did not have sex with, and put them in between the ones I did have sex with. The percent of time I'm having sex is pretty low. Keep in mind the margin of error is large because many have not been mentioned. I was only naked once in my life when I old a man no. The rest of the times, and several of the times I said I had sex, no clothing was removed. It was basically foreplay.

Some of my many Non-sexual Encounters with men and women (… no I'm not bi-sexual):

(Didn't get many invites from women) Did they not talk to me because they had something to hide? Didn't want the truth to be put on screen?

I recall a great relationship I had with a young man in middle school named Lamar. We talked about love and kissed each other when we were together. He lived on the same street as my then best friend Nicky; across the street from my cousin, the drummer, Bam Bam. His sister shares my name and later in life, after he married, his cousin became my boyfriend for a little while. Lamar and I wrote a lot of love letters back and forth to each other, but not during school. We mailed them. Or we handed them to each other after school. I mailed a pair of my underwear to him once and vice versa. We never had sex although one time I caught Nicky's bus home with her so that he and I could lay on each other and kiss and touch. My mother's best friend, who now works at the courthouse, told on me. She was and still is Nicky's father's lady friend. Guess who he married right out of high a school? My former friend, Dannyell. She was a cheerleader and I chose basketball. Girls playing basketball wasn't cool. Butch, (Charles Robinson), told me that. But I will always remember the beautiful banner Dannyell made for my birthday. The one she held up in the restaurant, in Paris where we were during (9th grade) Spring Break. I turned 15 and I was a virgin (completely; not half-way). I lost it soon after to my first love, Randy.

Andre was my first loves best friend. A few years after Randy and I broke up, Andre and I hung out in his home and watched TV and became good friends. I spent prom nite lying on the floor next to him. He didn't go with me. We kissed and one time he laid on me and we could have had sex but we didn't. We never removed any clothing.

Robert H., who moved to Europe to play B-ball years ago, was my boyfriend for a very short time during high school. We were both Basketball players at Largo. He came to my house once and I went to his house once. Both our parents were home each time. We kissed but we never touched without clothing and we never had sex. *He flew in from outer-space to sit next to me at the 20 year class reunion* but I knew he's already involved. We didn't dance or kiss. (How to Build a Better Boy).

I remember when my parents had a cabin in woods at a campground; I Fredericksburg. When we arrived, it ended up being a trailor on a small area of land, for camping. This was during high school. I invited my friend David and my friend Chandra to ride down with us to see it. It was a nice adventure. David was a year younger but he played ball at my school too. We never had a real kiss or had sex either. I will never forget the nite when he and I were watching the varsity boys play one time and he took his headphones off and reached over and put them on my head. Sunshine, by Babyface, was playing. That was sweet. I'm not sure what he's up to now. I also remember Chandra's dad taking us to Busch Garden's during high school years. She is now a surgeon.

I will always remember the Janet Jackson concert in which I had to pleasure of inviting Kenny, the editor at WTTG and musical genius, to attend with me, during high school. No kisses or anything. Just fun between friends.

I would be remiss to not mention the non-sexual encounters I had on –campus (at Towson) with guys who seemed to be rather aggressive toward me once invited into my room. Nothing happened between Raza and I nor with his friend Kyle. Nothing. As much as each of them tried. Nothing happened between me and my friend Chuck either. I really liked him. But again he was very aggressive regarding sex. But he was pretty much the only guy people would have seen me hanging with on campus.

After graduating, getting married, separated, and losing my job, I ended up working at a nite-club for about 5-6 months as a waitress. I had plenty of opportunities to fall. But I did not. I had one boyfriend that entire time. We went bowling and to a movie.

I visited Hampton University during this time for Homecoming and I ended up running into a guy who lived in the same area as Tim and Demond, (Scott is Demond's first name); who you will hear of later. He invited me and my friend over and his male friend Shante', our mutual friend from home, was in town too. His name is Stanley. He kissed me. I stopped it from going further. After I left is never pursued me. What does that tell you? I did not smell. He just wanted to see if he could get me to fall. But why? I didn't' carry myself that way, I didn't dress provocatively either. When I moved off-campus, Darryl from home and Russell from campus, each visited me at separate times. Nothing happened. Russell and I read the bible. But I could tell that Darryl was anticipating something. I'm not sure what.

It was my ex-husbands idea to go to the Poconos for our honeymoon. I never thought about my safety and I'm now glad that neither of us was mauled by a bear. We were deep in the woods in a beautiful, large cabin house. It was in an area where there were other homes but they weren't right next door.

I recall inviting my friend form high school, Nicky, to a
Yolanda Adams concert for her birthday once.
I also will never forget being inviting and attending the New
Year's concert at the Convention Center in DC with Chandra.
We brought in the new Millenium.
Jameille, my Christian soror from college, invited me to attend
an event at the Kennedy Center in DC. I had to get escorted
up the locked staircase because I do not ride elevators. I do not
remember the production.
I truly enjoyed my experience on my date with Demarcus
from work, years ago, at the Rainforest Café in Tysons.
I remember a visit at my apartment from my new friend
Ahmad from Pakistan. He brought me ice cream and he
kissed me. He was nice and he was gorgeous. No we didn't
have sex of any sort.
I remember working hard as an assistant manager one
Saturday at Enterprise Rent a Car. Terrance and I closed up
the store and drove to Ocean City for the rest of the day. My
only courtship from a Caucasian happened after I returned
home from my failed marriage as well. He is/was a
commercial Airline pilot. We went to a restaurant in
Georgetown called, Piccolos. We also went dancing at a club
in Georgetown. I eventually was invited to his home in
Alexandria where he sat next to me on the sofa. We talked for
a little while but he drank too much while I was there. I only
sipped as I always do. He was to aggressive so I left. I did not
feel comfortable. That was the last time we spoke.
If you read some of my other books, you may recall two other
Georgetown dates that I'd gone one. These were first dates
and now we did not kiss or touch in any way other than a hug
good nite. Remember from my Slander book, Omar, the
federal officer invited me to sleep in his grandma's basement.
Nope, didn't sleep with him either.

Oh, and that yellow dress that I wore to Ty's wedding reception; like the one a certain movie star wore in Roscoe Jenkins; is the dress I wore when I danced with Ty's light-skinned cousin, Terrance who earlier on, invited me into his room to tell me that since I was homeless, I could sleep in his room anytime. Nothing happened.

Kissed a woman once and sucked on her breast, never slept with her.

The same Federal Officer named Toni that showed up in my life when I'd lost my job in the school system, had previously visited my apartment years before. We worked together. (His part-time job). I sat on his lap, facing him on my sofa, fully clothed. We kissed then and he told me he was married. I instantly made him leave. No I've never slept with any police officers. This country is attempting, and so far they have been successful at orchestrating my life. The wanted me to run so that while I was forced to stay home and watch my grandson, while writing books, I would be "Gone Girl". I hadn't even seen the movie when I had business cards made to advertise my book (sells). The cards read: You are a witness to my murder if you do not buy my books. (They didn't buy my books and they were hoping that I would be murdered in jail for pan-handling.) I was not then, nor am I now pretending or hoping that someone murders me. I have no intentions of running with a warrant on my head. I'm not bitter or violent. And the Gone Girl story, is not true regarding my husband and I or anyone else in my family.

Sexual Encounters: (When I say I couldn't feel it; that means, it didn't go in. It wasn't hard).

Let me start by qualifying these relationships by stating how, when and where we met: Unfortunately, everyone believes that I had intercourse with these people and their penis was hard and we were going at it for hours. I guess they were expecting larger breast. In most cases, there was nothing happening. Yes I have breast. They just wanted more.
The man I speak with now more than any other, made a statement to me the last time we had sex, which was almost a year and a half go; (the last time I've had sex). He said, "You don't like sex, do you?" I didn't answer. I love people. I am addicted to loving people ad that has nothing to do with sex. I am kind natured and people gravitate toward that. The devil gravitates toward it too, in an attempt to destroy the 'loving people' addiction. This is not a physical addiction I'm speaking of. I didn't wait two weeks and then decide to sleep with these guys.

If Randy had married me at age 19, we would have been married now for about 22 years. We met at Wild World Amusement Park. We were very close but somewhere, something went wrong. We had a disagreement and I decided that we shouldn't go to prom together. That decision changed the course of my life forever. We went to the movies and to each other's homes and to the Amusement park together. We had sex more than once, he was my first, and yes I felt it. Dewayne's mother lived in the same small town where my mother grew up. They had a lot to discuss when she dropped me off and picked me up from his house. He ran long distance track for Largo. We met at Cavalier/Cavalette track club. I remember he pecked my lips in the middle of the commons area. I guess that let people know I wasn't gay. He and I were voted best all-around during superlative week, Senior year. He was my boyfriend for a short period. We went to church together once. Had he and I married at age 19, we would have been married now for about 22 years. He'll tell you we had sex for a minutes before my mother picked me up one day. I'll tell you we didn't. (With all of the interest from males in high-school, does it seem like they thought I may have been gay to you)?

Butch was actually Lamar's good friend. Lamar never asked me out or talked to me in high school, like Butch did. And although Butch and I didn't go on a date we attempted to have sex one day in my room when my parents were gone, but my vagina was closed, it didn't go in and we never tried again until many years later when I had my own apartment, after my divorce. He was just a guy who I could always talk to about anything and I was hospitable; (..in his eyes). After we went to the movies, he took me to his house so that I could meet this mom. His mother is an attorney. His family has money. I guess, I wasn't good enough. Didn't realize he just wanted to talk about me behind my back. He has a half-sister who shares my first name. She has a boy and a girl and she does hair. She's married. She has a nose like the Angela in the movie Why Did I Get Married? I don't believe she acts/drinks like that either.

I once had sex with a trucker whom I met in the shopping center where I did hair. He became one of my hair models. He had really pretty eyes. I braided his hair for my hair-book. We talked a lot while he was on the road. I expected the relationship to last. The one time we had sex it was in the sleeper part of his truck. It was exciting and fun. I wasn't doing it casually.

I met Fred in Human Resources at the State Department. I worked their one summer during and after high school. He did my finger-printing. He had a whole bunch of sister. They all lived in a big house in Southeast DC. They were really fun and nice. We hung out a lot. All of us sometimes. We had sex and yes, I felt it. He even came to visit me in college, when I lived off campus. He brought his friend Dave with him. My roommate at the time was Chandra. The four of us were snowed in and we played games, and cooked and had a good time. I gave him and his sister a ride one day but he lied about where we were going. After that, I never really trusted him anymore. It wouldn't have been a big deal, but he lied about it. I even invited him to church with me once. He went with me too. He and I had sex and yes I could feel it.

I met Stacy, at my church. He invited me to his home and I invited him to our cook-outs at my mom's. We both declared that we didn't want to have sex. So we didn't. We tried not to put ourselves in that position. But it ended up happening for about 5 minutes until we both felt convicted. We went to church, we met to eat and I don't remember what else. It seemed as if after the intimate moment, he didn't like me anymore. But during this time I left for college. He went off to Seminary school.

I met Kevin through a woman who worked at the post office, for my mother; (the supervisor). I guess they got to talking about their children and realized that we might hit it off, if we met. He and I sat on the sofa one day, talking to my mother and father. No we did not kiss. He actually was working in Prince George's County as a phlebotomist, but attending classes during the day at Morgan. He was sometimes able to give me a ride to school when I had traveled down to my parents; before I'd brought my car to school with me. Before I took my car the second year when I moved off campus. I don't remember anything that we did as far as dating is concerned but we were intimate once. I don't think he was as interested in me as I was in him. The relationship didn't last very long. Yes we had sex in my dorm room and yes I could feel it. Ryan was a guy who attended Towson. Our eyes met and I passed him a lot each time I would enter the main building on campus where the mail facility and conference rooms where located. It was a commons area as well. We actually exchanged numbers one day and later on after talking, he invited me over. I must say, I honestly accepted the invitation to his apartment off campus because I was bored. We could have had sex, but it never happened. We kissed, I laid on his bed. I removed clothing. I know if you ask him, he'll say he slept with me.

This is a great time to make my point. If Ryan had a girlfriend, why would he invite me over? I've never had hygiene problems, nor did I then. The only thing I can think of is that I laid down with this guy, too soon or that my breast weren't big enough. But why call me a ho? Not that he did, but, why would you think of the situation that way? Any other time on campus, the interaction was never sexual. I never removed clothing or anything. Why would guys say I did? I didn't carry myself that way nor was I aggressive toward them. I was attractive and I was focused.

Around this time in college, I met my husband. We kissed when we first met but it was awhile before we became intimate. He was traveling with the Redskins and I was very focused on graduating from school. I spent time in my room off-campus studying.

During my separation from my husband, a year and a half after we'd married, I went home to live with my parents. Timothy had been my friend since middle school years or so. He and I began to talk a lot on the phone. He'd relocated to North Carolina for college. I don't believe at that time he'd completed college but he was a barber to all the big ball players in college. He ended up opening his own Barbershop in Durham. At this time I was a just becoming a licensed stylist. We ran into each other intentionally in New York at the big Hair Show. No we did not have sex but we went to lunch and he gave me a ride home. I didn't have to ride the bus home with the other Cosmetology school students. We dated and he came home quite often. We eventually became intimate. He ultimately ended up telling me that he was now engaged to another female friend he had been seeing. The twist is that our mutual, friend, Scott; his best friend; was in love with me. He was a car salesman. He was still living in the area where we all grew up. He invited me out quite often. By this time, I'd lost all of my female friends and my career was not taking off. All of their careers were soaring.

When my husband and I divorced, I walked into the
barbershop stood in the middle of the floor and asked if
anyone could cut my hair. No one else wanted to do it. But
Mike, was willing. He wasn't the best looker, but he was a
talker. And I like to communicate. We exchanged numbers
and he tapered me a few more times before I began going to a
girl named MiMi who played B-ball at Largo when I was still
on JV. She was a senior. Mike eventually invited me out to a
movie. That night we had sex once in his very messy home.
Then he visited me once at my home and I felt he forced
himself upon me. I stopped talking to him.
This was about the time when I had my first one night stand;
(one, of the two I've had). Not by choice. I went to a party at
Howard University; alone because I have no female friends.
No one would talk to me. Not one woman. It was a fight
party. A naked stripper lay at my feet. I got up and moved. I
went into the room to watch the fight with the men. I still
hadn't found anyone to talk to. One guy tried to lure me
upstairs for sex. It didn't work. But right as I was headed for
the door, to leave, a young man struck up a conversation with
me. He walked out with me the invited me to his apartment. I
figured I was out and needed social interaction, so why not.
He lived on; the top floor. At that time I rode elevators. The
view was assume. We ended up having sex. This was the first
time I'd ever felt like this isn't cool; so soon. I felt like he
wasn't the one. I went home the next morning. I called and
called. He had no intentions of talking to me again. I showed
up at his door and he was terrified. All I will say is, I will
never attend that school. Never. He said his name was Heath.
I was setup by my former girlfriend, Hollywood and a
Historically Black University.

At this point I had everything I needed except for a large savings account. I was already a Christian. I had my own place, my own car, a decent job, I was traveling using my own paycheck and I was in control of my daughters schooling. Although I wasn't using my degree; and that made my resume look strange. I wasn't focused on that then. To busy trying to keep a roof over my head. (Here's to jobs that pay the bills).

During this time I worked briefly for Bell Atlantic. I drove a gold car and my boyfriend, Chris, who had a very big, white American Bulldog. He rode a motorcycle. He rode up next to me and asked for my number. He dropped me at work and kept my car. He lived in an efficiency in Southeast DC. He was very sexy and extremely nice. I loved his dog. He had hair like an Arab and his penis was a very nice size. He had the most beautiful deep brown skin like a Middle-Eastern guy. I think when you have small breast you may unconsciously turn to have sex from behind. I was so busy with work and I knew he was too, therefore I became content just spending a little time in his home and walking the dog with him. He drove me to work every day. I sat in his barbershop sometimes just to see how his day went. He eventually opened his own shop. I never entered his bedroom because I never intended to have sex but he would kiss me wherever we were and then it would happen. Kneeling on the sofa or standing at the table.

When I was living in my apartment complex, I was approached by a guy with long locs. He asked if he could call me. We exchanged numbers and he called. He was a barber who worked I the shop across the street from my apartment. I often would stop by and sit in to talk to him when I was either coming or going. I know that I that field, you spend a lot of time at work. We sat and looked at magazines when he didn't have clients. I don't believe we ever went on a real date. Probably too soon, he came to my apartment I guess looking back he was trying to prove that I was easy. Why would someone with locs want to do that? His calls seemed to get fewer and fewer after we had sex. I actually teared up, it felt so good. But that wasn't my goal. Having satisfying sex was not my purpose. Oh well, he didn't mean me any good. So that ended.

It was during this time that someone wearing my yellow hat and my dad's flip glasses, on the show, A Different World, made the world "aware" that either my father or myself, needed prune cobbler, and someone had a coach-roach in their living room. (I didn't grow up with roaches or mice). The only female visitor I had brought my daughter a very nice coat for Christmas. It seemed as if Tara stopped by to also check for roaches. I recall her standing in the middle of the room looking around. I only saw a bug when it rained but eventually I left for that reason. I guess it's just ironic that my husband's girlfriend from middle school was in that particular TV show. The next movie I saw her in, had a Native American woman using my name, wearing my dress, toting a gun in her purse, smoking a cigarette. I've never owned a gun and I've never smoked.

Somewhere during this time, I called Erik B, my good friend
from high school and we had sex. Long story short. I was
invited to go to the Aquarium in Baltimore with Lamar's
cousin, Maurice. We went to lunch, hung out at his apartment
and he told me that he had traveled to a lot of places. I
thought that meant he was very serious about me. We dated,
we spent time together. But ultimately, he stopped calling.
I moved back home and of course this allowed me to run into
guys whom I'd grown up with. When I left for college, I had
not slept with anyone in my neighborhood. Over the next
several years the number became three. I'd known these guys
since early elementary. Two of them said they had been
divorced like me. One had kids, one didn't. The other guy had
recently returned home from school in North Carolina. We
went to the movies and he invited me to his home for a small
cook-out. I spent a lot of time watching TV with him in his
basement. And we went to church together with his mother.
But something wasn't right. He wasn't the friendly guy he
used to be in school. I went to lunch and to church with the
other Bryan also. Brian B, Bryan R and Tallion or Elliott, most
called him. Now, many years later, if you ask them why they
didn't marry me, they say that I was a ho. These weren't one
nite stands and we know each other's stories and families for
over 25 years. Why play games? Why would any Black man
want to use any Black woman for sex. Especially one who
you've known all your life. All three of them "got blowjobs".
Something I hadn't 'learned to do' until that particular time;
not even with my own husband. I just saw it as a part of the
love we made. It was my idea.

During this time I attended a job fair in Tyson's Corner. I ended up with an interview with Enterprise rent a car. They had a Management Training Program that guaranteed you a starting salary of $30,000. During this time I had lunch with Kevin S. and took a bus trip with him and his friends to Delaware to a casino. I went with him and his friends to a concert at Bull Run Park. After all this. He tried to hook me up with his friend after telling me he was taken. I'd already had sex with him. He worked at the car dealer next door to my job. I had sex with a married man in his office in Sligo Creek. I knew he was married but I assume that if he was coming on to me, and it went that far, that he had no intentions on staying married. He was not my superior. We never worked together in any office. I worked in a different region. His name was Cortez. I went over to a guys house whom I'd worked with before, to visit and ended up snowed in. The rest of my extended family had gone ahead and driven up the mountain to Pottstown Pennsylvania for a family sleepover. I had to work that day for 4 hours at Enterprise and they left earlier the morning. Everybody. I usually attended all family functions. I decided not to drive up alone. I carefully drove home. But not before me and Mike F. had sex. He said something really mean. He knew that I had a relationship for almost a year with a guy named Antoine when I was working there. He and I lived together. We both had little girls. My parents and he and I and our children went to the company picnic together. I ended up breaking up with him. He'd wanted to marry me. He took me to a professional basketball game. When we were together, I'd gotten pregnant and it was no secret. I ended up getting my first and only abortion. Mike told me to move before I get pregnant again. After that I left; his house and the company. It was time for me to find a new job. I had worked my way up to Assistant Manager. It was a great experience. As a matter of fact, one of my employees came to my apartment so that I could assist him with studying for his Assistant Manager test that would move him from

Trainee up to the next level. No I did not sleep with him.
After this I ran into two guys I knew from high school. Floyd
and Mike B. Floyd came to my apartment to tell me that
someone had stolen his car, I prayed with him. I even went to
Seat Pleasant and asked around to see if anyone knew about
what had happened to his car. I even invited him to come and
he accepted my invitation to see Maxwell in concert. Only to
show up unannounced at his home one day to find him
cheating on me. (Maybe they'd heard that I'd had sex with
more than one guy at the same job). These relationships didn't
turn into marriage either. Well, why pretend that you are
saving the day? Why waste my time? AND I DID NOT
SMELL!!

At this point (in my mind) the guy who looked like the man
from Brown Sugar; the movie, who sang, "the ho is mine";
was my friend Demond (Scott). He'd told everyone that he
and I were going to be married. He says we had sex, I say we
didn't. I still love him though. Although his mother had
helped me get my DOD job when I was a teen, and I truly
cared for him and his family. I had to say, no thanks.

I worked. I was a single-mom. I hadn't seen the movies that
everyone else had seen. The movies that told a story about
"me" or so they believed. The relationship was doomed. Their
intentions were not good from the beginning. Males and
females stopped being my friend. The campaign against me
was overwhelming. I wasn't pressed them and I'm not now.
It's 2015. I never knew that people thought the woman who
dropped her boyfriend off in Barbershop, was me. It's been
said, that guys only liked me for my butt. No man has ever
grabbed my butt during intimacy. Do you want to imagine
them on top or that they just aren't very sexually inclined. Not
even my husband, except before we married. It's like the
woman in the movie, The Help. She says the women don't like
her because of something that they "believed" she did.

After seven years, I was fired from the school system for smacking a boy on the arm. They struck me while fighting in my classroom- After verbally harassing me for 7 years; and that didn't make me resign. From here on, I am unemployed for the most part. But I am definitely homeless. Living in a different hotel each school year. The hotels had kitchens so I was able to cook for my daughter. I pan-handled to pay for the hotel and everything else. Now we might lose our storage. Every memory I know of my mother and my life. I didn't have one child in 7 years to say "Ms.Williams you smell funny". Not one teacher or administrator. I've never had a family member say I smell until this past Thanksgiving. (2014). Now there's a worldwide campaign to say I smell. The entire time that I was in the school system, I had one sex partner from within the school system. My boyfriend, or at least I thought. Mr. Little (Dewayne), was his name. He is the only man who has ever come to my home I the middle of the nite. He left around 3:30 in the morning. I've never gone to or left anyone's home I the middle of the nite and no man has ever some to see me or left, in the middle of the nite. When I lost my career in 2008/09 I had 5 different male visitors who seemed to want to try to make me fall. No there was no touching or kissing or anything: Mr. Chamberlain; Toni the Federal agent; Reggie from my old neighborhood; and Mr. Goldstein or Mr. Cameron from the last school where I worked.

I was homeless for seven years. I've had seven forced sex partners. And one husband of a relative. But I'm to blame. I don't think so. And yes I believed his marriage was already over. This happened two years after we became homeless. That is not the reason why I was left homeless. I expected dating and marriage each time, sometimes I dated sometimes I didn't. I don't ever have sex with you if I don't love you. Left homeless with a child, by Christians and non-Christians. I have no desire to worship with any of them. But I know the word says do not forsake the assembly with like believers. They must not believe the same thing I do. (One of these 7 men is the one still talking to me on Facebook because I don't have a phone). EV. "Welcome to my wicked world"? Whatever. Welcome to his. Now he's not talking to me either. I don't use the word ho, typically but if I were you I would save it for arguments regarding someone who has multiple children by multiple mates or someone who knows you don't want to marry them but they think you make them cum all the time so they just want you for sex. I would also save that term for those who focus on becoming rich until they're 40 then desperately seek a husband or instantly become pregnant to beat the clock. I wouldn't make that argument against someone who found Jesus at an early age, joined a Christian sorority in college, married young and volunteered in their community. All while dealing with slanderous lies about their character in movies and TV; as they attempted to date. I'm very happy single; for life, because I know I'm not a slut. Nor have I ever been. Through all of the street rumors and TV lies, I now the truth.

I'm convinced that no matter what your profession or race, most people out here, Christian or not, are not very bright. And even meaner than they are dumb. "I was a ho but now I'm waiting;" their saying. Could they be any dumber? I'm not too easy. They are so pathetic that they want the world to believe that they are telling me what to do in my life, even down to what I write about. To me that says they are extremely desperate and insecure. I'm not looking for a man. When I say I didn't smell, I'm not implying that I was always actually having the intercourse and could have smelled. Most of these encounters were not what you think. No penetration whatsoever. My breath didn't smell either.

They are trying to force me to be in love with a man by making sure that he is literally the only soul on earth talking to me. Then they say I'm violent. I'm not. But you deserve violence for lying on me all of these years, Hollywood Films. Somehow I've gone through 16 years of school, a marriage and plenty of relationships after my divorce, before oral sex came into play. Now, according to all men; it's what I'm none for. Yawl are some trifling folks. I wanted true love; forever in ever encounter. ALMOST DOESN'T COUNT.

It's a conspiracy.

Can I earn a living please?

My daughter lost her job today. Now what are we gonna do?

This is an excerpt from my book: Libel and Slander of Angela Williams-

My School-Aged Years

I haven't always been homeless. In fact I lived a great childhood and my early adult life started out plush and very eventful. One might say I felt very lucky; blessed even.
It was a neighborhood with two entrances. Neither had a sign that let a driver know that they had arrived. You were now in Ritchie Manor off of Ritchie Road; where the children went to Ritchie Elementary and in my home, they lived on Richville Drive and watched the cartoon, Richie Rich. Our house was small but it had 4 bedrooms and 1 ½ bathrooms. No dishwasher, no fireplace and no pantry. I can only speak for our household when I say. We weren't rich, but we didn't want for anything. Oh, and did I tell you that Woody Wood Pecker lived behind my house? ("No"). Well, he did.
Our neighborhood was full of young kids who enjoyed playing together. My house was in the back of the neighborhood on the last street. Our house was in the middle of our street. There was no house directly across from us so when we hosted our large family for cook-outs, there was always somewhere to park. The location of our home was great for kick-ball and dodge ball. The sidewalk was perfect for double- dutch and roller skating. There was only one thing we had to worry about. The neighborhood terror. This new family moved in two doors down and brought this frightening German Shepard. You would think that they would have purchased a thicker chain or a taller fence. For ten years, he popped his chain and chased the nearest person into a frenzy. He actually bit a few people. You wanna know his name? He has the same name as the toy doll who comes to life and stabs his victims to death. He has the same name as the big mouse with the pizza adventure land for, children's birthdays.

We had a dog for a little while when I was 5. He used to pop his chain too but he didn't bite people. Eventually, he ran away. I guess looking back, they were both scared of the animals in the woods behind our homes.

My mother always had birthday parties for me and my brother. It's warm during my birthday and it falls near a holiday and sometimes Spring Break. We would usually not have trouble getting the entire family to come to a cook-out during a holiday; and even our numerous family friends.

My mother used to manage a bank and believe it or not she used to take me to work with her when I was really little; I remember. She was good friends with a lady from India. She shared the name of the puppy on the cartoon Arthur. It was really fun. She eventually left to work for the postal service, like my father. He's worked the night shift ever since I could remember. My mother worked her way up to supervisor but he chose to keep his position and shift. I'm saddened when I think that neither me nor my brother were in a position to take care of our parents the way they took care of us. But at least they had each other after we left.

Although my mom was not a haunted Plymouth vehicle, she drove very fast. That is her name. Christine, like the movie. She called her bosses, Boss and she was married to a mouse whom she could never catch, in a silent cartoon. Yes that's my dad's name. Well it's just like the ocean...under the moon...; no my brother is not a Spanish singer but he shares his first name. (Give us your heart, make it real or just forget about it).

Our parents worked hard but they played hard too. They loved to travel. When we were young, they took us everywhere. We had a conversion van that allowed us to take road trips in comfort, before gas prices were high and unstable. When we were very young, we flew once and drove down a few years later, to Sea World and Disney World in Orlando, Florida. After my mother's brother was relocated to Wisconsin by his employer, we drove way up there to visit. When I was ten and my brother was sixteen, we drove in a caravan with two other families from the neighborhood, to the World's Fair in New Orleans, Louisiana. Our male cousin who share the name of the son on *The Fresh Prince*, went with us. Everybody had a riding partner. My father or brother rode with me. I forgot to tell you why I couldn't get in the pool at the hotel. A week or so before our trip, I was riding my ten speed with the girl who invited me to play basketball, on the back of my bike. We got up our speed so that when we passed the house with the big dog, we would just sail on by. I didn't work out that way. He was in the front and his bark scared me so much that I crashed my bike. She walked home and I walked my bike home. Bloody and scarred, (obviously discombobulated), I tucked myself into bed. My brother was in his room and my dad was downstairs watching TV. When my mom got home she came in my room and I was bloody and scarred. She yelled at both of them. I couldn't remember where we fell; she asked me. We had to go get my friend and she told my mom what happened. (I didn't have restrictions as to where I could ride within the neighborhood. I wasn't lying. I truly didn't remember). I'm not a doctor so I didn't know that I needed x-rays and a scan of my brain. I had stitches and a big giant bandage on my side. My mom keep it clean and changed my bandage regularly but my trip was not quite as fun as it probably could have been. But it's OK because my brother and I had a lot of stuff around the house to keep us busy. We played cars, Battleship, Connect Four and even had out own arcade sized pinball machine. Every Friday our parents bought dinner from a different carry-out and sometimes we would play Bingo.

Speaking of stiches; my former friend, the surgeon; sister of the anesthesiologist, used to play dolls and house with me and the girls in my neighborhood. Me, her and another little girl, were lying on the ground pretending to be in bed and I needed more space, so I told her to roll-over. She fell down from ground level to the bottom of the basement steps, right in front of the basement door. She busted her chin. We had to rush her to the emergency room. You would think that experience led her to become a doctor but not quite.

Two of my mother's female friend's had a devastating health issue at a much younger age. Fortunately, they survived. The mother of these two previously mentioned doctors, had an aneurism. The mother of the young woman whose first name is my middle name; had breast cancer. They are both still alive and well.

A few years later, for a couple of weeks during the summer, my mom and dad sent me and my brother (alone on a plane) to visit her other brother and his family in Melbourne, Florida. Although he lived in Greece many years before he was stationed in Melbourne, we didn't fly overseas as a family to visit.

I ended up going to Europe in the 9th grade with the French Club. I was taking Spanish, but it was an opportunity that I didn't want to miss. I celebrated my 15th birthday in Europe. It was great. I've never been attacked by a bidet-(*BAPS*). I've never fallen in love with one either- (*Jumping the Broom*). I'd never seen one and I used it once when we first got there. My super fantastic moment of celebration can actually be matched by a super scary moment when I left my purse on the train; in (I believe it was), Switzerland. As I exited the train, I realized my purse was not with me. It had my traveler's checks inside. I don't remember if our chaperone held on to all of our passports or not, but I ran back down the platform and onto the train. I was frantic hoping that the train didn't pull off. I grabbed my purse and rejoined my group. In hind-sight I guess being separated from my group and lost in another country would have been much worse than replacing my traveler's checks.

Both sides of my family has always had family reunions on a fairly regular basis. My father's side more frequently than my mom. I don't know which is true. My mother's side of the family stopped having reunions after my mom passed away or after my younger female cousins got married. I think they are all keeping their men locked away for safe keeping.

My father's, mother's, brother's, wife (or his aunt, through marriage) is still living and we are still in touch with that extended family. Meet them. May I introduce them? I only eat the Brown M&M's cause chocolates already Brown. They are very nice and they are all very accomplished. (Mind you; that is the last name of the young lady whose birthday is on September 11th; and my grandmother's maiden name). Our reunion is always the weekend of my grandmother's birthday. I guess I'll see them this fall. Here's the catch. My only nephew graduates from high school this spring near Tampa. If I ride down there with my dad and stay so that I can move to Miami near my brother I won't make it to my grandson's first family reunion. Who will watch my grandson?

When I was in elementary school, my father's dad was found dead on the sidewalk out-side of his home. He had apparently fallen or been thrown from his high-rise apartment window. I've never read the police report, however I wouldn't be surprised to find conflicting evidence. Could the movies, Beverly Hills Cop and I Robot be eluding to the need for a new investigation.

If you are a parent; whether you're obese or not, and you over heard your fifth grader on the phone talking about her boyfriend, would you be devastated. If you had a fifth grader who ate twice as much food during each meal, as your other children; would you be concerned. What if he or she didn't eat vegetables? What about smoking cigarettes or drinking alcohol? Are either of these reasons to stop either child from participating in extracurricular activities? You may not stop them but you definitely need to encourage them. Please keep in mind as you read; I do not have any addictions, nor have I ever. I've never smoked anything or abused alcohol or drugs.

I was invited to go to basketball practice with a friend of mine from the neighborhood when I was 9 years old. (A friend who shares the same last name as the scary family who named their daughter Wednesday). From that day forward I was hooked on the game. (Or maybe I was hooked on all the new friends and fun I was now having). Every season I played a sport with the community Boys and Girls Club. When football time rolled around; I cheered. I played basketball in the winter and softball in the summer. A lot of times, my mother, carpooled a lot of us to practice. We were really good. We had two coaches and one of them was, my (former) best friend and team-mates; father. Our other coach was an older white man who owned a property in Ocean City. Every summer he took three of us to the beach for a weekend. Including our other coach's daughter of course. Life was fun. I only wished I had encouraged my brother to get involved in Boys and Girls Club activities. I wonder why no young men invited him. I wonder what prompted her to invite me.

My mom took us to see Ice Capades every time they came into town.

My mother was like the team mom. She even got an award for being so dedicated to our team; during boys and girls club and high school. My dad worked at night so he missed all of my High school basketball games. The year I ran track; he traveled with us everywhere.

My mom loved to shop. I remember keeping a calendar on my wall logging every outfit; being sure not to wear anything twice in one month during high school. Even when I was smaller I was particular about my outfits. I recall walking through a department store with my mom wearing my all purple outfit to match my newly painted bedroom. (I asked if they could paint my room purple). I was walking with her and she said, "Where is your other shoe?" I said, "It's back there stuck in the escalator." My new, purple Jordache sneaker. We went back to get it. I believe I was in the fourth grade.

I remember in elementary school when my mother bought her first dream car. She and my brother picked me up from 6th grade, in a really nice, brand-new, BMW. Unfortunately, my dad totaled it. (Not before my former friend, the Anesthesiologist, used it for her high school prom. But the important thing is that he is OK. His rib broke and punctured his lung. (The actor/actress is driving my mother's car in the movie Machete).

I remember my mother dropping me and my life-long neighbor and friend, (the spice from Gilligan's Island), at bible study on some Sundays. She and I played Barbie dream house in our basements on numerous occasions. We got our first ten-speed bikes on the same Christmas.

The dark side of my basement will always be like the dark side of the moon to me. (.....nothing to do with Mulan). I could never reach my arm around and turn on the light for fear that the monster would get my arm. So I would always fall to sleep on the couch and my brother would come downstairs, pick me up, put me in the bed and tuck me in.

I was taking a lot of dance classes at a small Fashion Institute that was preparing me to compete in the MISS TEEN Pageant; where I won 1st runner up; I was 14. Having the support of an entire community of friends, family and my parents' co-workers, was an awesome feeling. It almost felt surreal, being on stage with that many people clapping for you. (Angelica from the movie; *Six Days, Seven Nights;* my talent: my dance and my out-fit). Well, my hips aren't narrow anymore and my breast may actually be big enough now, too bad I don't look like her. Maybe I could have snagged my green-eyed friend from Wild World Amusement Park.

Oh yeah. That was my first job ever. I met a lot of people. Including my first love. I saw him and wanted to meet him. I was introduced and as I glanced at the other guys in the landscaping department, I immediately became overtaken by another guy. This green-eyed hunk. But it was too late. I composed myself and began a great love affair with the guy who was just as excited to meet me. Guess what happened. My new boyfriend, offered me a ride home. Great! Not great. The gorgeous hunk, was his best friend. He was riding home with us. No I didn't cheat. He was an OK boyfriend. Our mothers talked to one-another and everything. During the summer, he took me to the movies and a few times we returned to work on our day off, to enjoy the fun of the amusement park. Our mother's visited with each other and everything.

He even came to my first dance in high school. I don't remember him inviting me to any of his dances. Our relationship was strained because he didn't attend the same school as I did. Everyone was telling me that he had cheated on me with a girl at his school. They told me her name and everything. I think he must have been just flirting with her. (Oh, a plan to break us up-*High School Musical*). When I wasn't in school I was busy with sports. He was busy in the spring with baseball. They both played for their school. Something in my heart felt different. (Maybe he was mad because he was really overdressed at the Back-To-School Dance). I didn't know he was going to be all dressed up. He never invited me to go out anymore. After a year or so he and I broke up but we were still friends. I had a few other boyfriends during high school. Those relationships didn't last very long. I'm not sure what was said. We talked for a while once and I'm sure we entertained getting back together. But me and my first love ended up 'breaking up for good', (on the phone), right before the prom. I didn't cheat on him or anyone else. (Might not make sense to you, but it's the world of teen-agers). I decided that we shouldn't go to the prom together. I ended up going alone.

{He led the Redskins to victory in Super Bowl 22. (Just say his name over and over out loud to yourself). I had not long before, had sex for the first time in my life, with my boyfriend-(my first love). But my father sure watches a lot of sports on TV. He could probably draw out some plays. He even looks a little like him}. OMG. So this is the other reason why my high school coach gave me his daughter's jersey number; 22?

For the next year or so, I became closer friends with my ex's best friend. We talked on the phone. It was a while before I actually went over to his home. I think it all started when I found myself talking to him about being mad at my boyfriend years ago when he made me mad.

On prom night, I went to dinner at a restaurant on the water, with a group of friends, (other couples); before the Prom. Guess who I danced with during the first slow song? My Physics teacher. I thought I looked great and I felt beautiful. It was a great night. I went to a Prom after party at a hotel. It wasn't really my scene so I didn't stay long. Then I went to my green-eyed friend's house so he could see how pretty I looked. We slept on the basement floor in front of the TV; fully clothed, all nite; he snuck me in. No we didn't touch. The next morning I went home changed my clothes and went to Kings Dominion with the same group of friends of which I'd gone to the pre-Prom dinner.

Well, he moved to Florida and opened a Fitness Gym. Did I mention that the one and only time he came to my house, when high school was ending; he brought me a roll of cookie dough. He walked in, handed it to me and walked right back out? Yes I knew and still know how to make cookies in the oven, the proper way; I don't need Ingrid from Uptown Girls, to show me. *Clueless.* They're both married; and have been for some time now. Well, anyway....Maybe I'll see him and his family when I go visit my brother. Maybe I won't. Maybe I'll run into my ex when I'm 50, and he'll be single; I doubt it because the last time I ran into him, he was really rude. I'm not sure why. When I ran into him while pan-handling a few years back he came to my hotel and played scrabble with me. Back to b-ball with my girls:

When it was time for high school, many of us were used to playing ball together so we won a lot of games even though we were short. We made it to the State Championship all four years. We made it; but we came in second every time. (Our coach always said "No one ever remembers who comes in second"). *Welcome Home Roscoe Jenkins.* I don't know what they feed those Broadneck girls; they were all ginormous!

I recall my girlfriend's, sister's boyfriend moving to Colorado. She shares the name of the daughter of the 42nd President. He was in the Air Force and that was where he was stationed. She decided to attend college out there to be near him. Me and my girlfriend flew out to visit her sister during our spring-break. Colorado is absolutely breath-taking. And although her relationship didn't work out and she had a baby before she finished college, she completed medical school on the East-Coast and is now an Anesthesiologist. You go girl!

My mother's friend worked for an entertainment company and was able to get her tickets to some major concerts. During the last two years of high school, during college and a few years after college; me and my mom, were blessed enough to get great seats to the concerts of, Janet Jackson, Michael Jackson and Maxwell. My mother and I went to see Michael but I was able to invite a friend to go with me to see the other artists.

Even though I didn't accept the basketball scholarship to Salisbury, I played intramural basketball at Towson, for fun and exercise. Ok, I should have known to join a media club of some sort even if I wasn't guided to do so. I guess I hadn't really decided what part of Mass Comm I'd desired to work. I remember speaking with my green-eyed friend who was attending Hampton. He shared with me that he would be transferring to another college because his current school did not have his particular major.

I decided to join a Christian Sorority called ANQ. I recall driving down to Atlanta, Georgia to a Christian Conference with 3 of my frat brothers and 3 of my sorors. There was a snow storm brewing, but we'd already paid our money so we took our time and took turns driving the minivan we'd rented. I was friends with a lot of male and female freshmen on campus. But the new, third-string, freshman quarterback introduced me to my husband. He said we sounded a lot alike when it came to the things of God. No I did not allow him to spend the night. We spent the majority of our time hanging out in my apartment and working out on the track. My soon to be husband, was too busy anyway. He was in and out of town and focused on trying to become a pro-ball player. He was a cornerback. He left school, before graduating to play on the Redskins practice squad. He only had 11 credits to go but that was a chance of a life-time. His jersey number was 22. My jersey number was 22.

During this period, my parents were traveling a lot. Long cruises to the cost of Mexico and other Islands; a trip to Alaska, a trip to Africa. And a train ride across country. Thanks *Home Alone* for the credits that may have led my mom to travel. Who knew she would get sick at such a young age.

Now during my relationship with my soon to be husband, I was very focused on graduating. He was traveling and trying to land a contract with the Redskins. I was wondering why I hadn't been invited to meet his mom and dad yet. Come to find out, his ex-girlfriend had fought with her mom and was staying at his mother's. (He lived there too). His parents didn't know for a long time that there was someone else. He called me from LA one night talking 'bout SHE was with him and she said she was pregnant. I cried for months. He had taken her to the Redskins cook-out while he was supposed to be with me. By the way, you know that girl who sucked the former president's penis; yeah, that was his ex-girlfriends name. (Is that what he wanted from me?) Come to find out, she wasn't pregnant and she left him when he got cut from the Redskins practice squad. He showed up a year later at my door, with flowers; in tears. Against my friends and family member's advice, I took him back. He didn't even have a job. I graduated and found a job as a Reprographics Assistant in the Graphics Department of an Architect firm. I told him that if we were going to continue having sex and he wanted to spend the night, we had to get married. But we planned our wedding. Three months later I was pregnant. I named my daughter after the character in *Mo' Better Blues*. (I was not pregnant when I got married). No, the movie wasn't about me and I've never been to Harlem, but I was dark skinned, and I'd won. It's so sad that things happened the way they did. I, (we), gave up on our marriage so soon. (I wish we'd traveled to an island or taken a cruise for our honeymoon). We went to the Poconos. Can you blame me for trying to form a solid marriage union at an early age?

The new Cinderella movie just came out last week. The light-skinned actor from Mo' Better Blues, shares my last name; in real-life. So I guess she is the real Cinderella. Cause I'm still single. Lol. Maybe I'm still single because an actor/actress whose name in real–life happens to be the same as mine, said in a movie called Waiting to Exhale; when asked about her failed marriage by a fellow actor, that she was not about to go out and find herself a new owner.

Speaking of failed marriage; I suppose the theme song, "Are you that special someone?", from Dr. Doolittle (1998) and the name Blossoms Mammoth Circus; has nothing to do with me being hurt by men who didn't take a relationship with me, seriously (After my divorce). I just noticed the Mammoth Circus scene at the end of the movie, today. May, 2015.

Back on campus:

It seemed as if those who didn't come to school with their best friends, became best friends with their room-mates. My room-mate was from my high-school but, unfortunately she didn't make the grades and lost her scholarship. She was smart but she became a sweetheart to a frat boy and the rest is history. She ended up leaving. She ended up at a larger University and has since graduated and is doing fine. My closest girlfriends had gone to school at Hampton and at MD Eastern Shore where there were a lot of guys from our area and our high school. I wonder if any of my friends ever fell sexually with any of them. I'm kind of surprised that it took them so long to find a life-mate and to have children.

I ended up with a nice White room-mate when I moved off campus. One of my sorors introduced us. She was barely home because she took a job as a nanny for a couple of young children in a neighboring county. I think I sort of pushed her away when I tried to minister to her one day. When she was home, her boyfriend from Bethany Beach was there too. A very attractive black guy. He spent the night quite often. That is not why I ministered to her though.

I remember my parents driving up to my gospel choir concert. It was really nice. My mom also drove up for my induction into the sorority. My pharmacist friend and her mom drove up for the induction as well.

My brother had sort of been coerced into enlisting in the military. He joined the Marines. I know he doesn't regret it. I remember going to his Graduation Ceremony in Parris Island, South Carolina. Soon after, he was stationed in Yuma, Arizona. He told me it was so hot there that you could see the heat rising from the ground. He might as well had been stationed in Africa!.... Well, not quite. You can't take a cross-country road trip home, from Africa. Can you believe he caught the bus home! (One day I hope to drive my daughter cross country to see the west coast). (According to her, she doesn't fly). He'd decided to get out of the military. He married shortly before me but we had our child shortly before them. Long story short, neither marriage worked out.

I was home, he was home, and my entire family came from miles around; crossed states even; to celebrate my daughters first birthday (It was my mother's sister's birthday too). My brother was the clown at her party. That was the theme. It was a cook-out. My daughter's father was there too. Unfortunately my husband didn't take the opportunity that posed itself, to try to rekindle our flame, other than attempting to sleep in the same bed with me. It was clearly over. Can you believe his mother called me talking bout' "he has needs". Not, He loves you and we should try to work it out by going on vacation; but, "he has needs". No, I did not have sex with him.

Now if you think that all of the situations with womanizers in college and the negative outcome with my marriage should make me aware of how volatile relationships with guys can be, you have to wonder why I only am able to have male friends after I return home from a failed marriage. A group of girlfriends rallying around me and helping me thrive again would have been very appropriate. Can't say I didn't try to make that happen.

Apparently, my brother couldn't find a permanent place to live (until he could get back on his feet). Not one family member. I don't remember saying he couldn't live with me and I had literally just gotten keys to my apartment. He and his wife had a son the same age as my daughter and they had recently broken up as well.

I know my brother's heart must have been broken and I feel bad. When a black male has one or two negative things happen in the early part of his life; he can definitely begin life with a defeated attitude.{ Especially if two of those things are as important as finding shelter, (character) / criminal record due to something minor as traffic violations (…this was years ago), or finance (bad credit). I'm just saying; in general, with black men….}

He left for Miami. He never moved back to this area. The tears of a clown-when no one's around. I might be cute but I ended up just being a substitute; deep inside I'm blue? Somebody's psychic, Lol. I hope to live near him one day, he's a good guy.

Deep down in my gut I have a feeling that my brother's sabotage is worse than mine. He told me that he had his own place and a job when he first got there. (He lost his job and never got back on his feet-"he didn't say this to me"-it's just plain to see). He can't work either. (Unfortunately he wasn't keeping in touch with me enough for me to know that his situation had become dire). It's probably because people are harassing him about his sister being a ho. Which I'm not. He has switched rolls with his girlfriend. She works while he stays at home. Sounds like my current life to a 'T'. Well, not to a 'T' cause I'm single. But my daughter thinks she's in the parent roll, because she's working and I'm not. I'm quite sure that no matter where my brother lived; Maryland or Florida; he would not have been able to pan-handle like I'm doing without being beaten by the cops. (When I hadn't heard from him, I went looking for him). I'm a woman and I found myself toe to toe with men who carry guns, (cops); a few times. I guess he and I both are the designated homeless. It's funny because they all think we're jealous of them, (family and friends). Why would everyone be so mean to me and my brother?

I recall flying down to my uncles because we hadn't heard from my brother. I asked my uncle to drive me to Miami. I found my brother in a shelter. He drove back to Melbourne with us. I figured he would be OK from that day forward. By the time I got back home, I understand that he ended up back to Miami. I tried to help. I was living with my parents then. We have all really let my brother down. He was never a menace to society either. (Was I the one who'd found someone who didn't have anything and put em' off on family; family that now live in Newport?) – *Soul Food*. It is a relatively old movie. It would have to be some deep, deep sabotage to try to make scenes from **this movie**; come true. You and I both know, I would never be drinking to get drunk (I don't drink beer) and I would never go after someone else's husband; especially in their home. I don't drink beer. They wanted it to come true so badly, that their husband comes after me. Me and my daughter became homeless because I lost my job. You should never have forced me to move up there.

If I was the person they say. I would be rich from "ho-ing" or stripping. I am not a ho now, nor did I used to be. I just found out what "tricking" meant not too long ago.

OK I know he doesn't consider himself homeless anymore. He found love. I guess homelessness is a little different for military veterans. I hope so.

He loves his family. My brother was never violent in school or in our home. I've visited him several times and even tried to relocate once. I just didn't have the means or the money to do so. I love him. I truly miss him. I hope to live near him one day. He never joined any sports programs or joined any organizations in grade school but he is a very smart, kind person. I failed to mention that I cried all the way home after visiting him in 2004. I did not want to leave him.

Our Christmas' were grand. My mother was a giver. During the earlier part of the year, my brother used to always say something and then say sike. So one Christmas, I got a little box and wrapped it just for him. The only thing it contained was a note stating the word, sike. We all cracked up laughing. (His son sort of reminds you of the guy in the TV show Psyche). And the big brother's T-shirt has nothing but the word sike on the front in the movie- *Diary of a Wimpy Kid*. He and I got along for the most part. We definitely didn't fight like the two boys in this series of movies. Although he didn't used to be the best driver; that is definitely not him in Diary of a Wimpy Kid. He purchased a used old-timer car; you know the thick heavy kind. Unfortunately the brakes gave out and he ran into a police car. (Columbiana). That sounds like a very big ticket to me. If you can't pay your ticket they revoke your license. If you have no license, you have no job. I guess you have to use your personal documents to get a personal identification card. Which may not be as easy as it sounds. But still probably looks bad to an employer. I'm sure this was just the beginning of his problems.

I'm glad that my brother's son had such a fun and rewarding experience in grade school but it breaks my heart to know that my brother wasn't able to be a part of it. Anyone in a position to change his situation, should have. You can't get those precious moments back. Maybe they'll be closer now that his son is older and able to drive himself around.

I'm saddened to think that I can't get the time back that I've lost being so far away from my brother but I can only pray that we will see each other again and be able to enjoy each other's company for however long we have.

Some time ago I began a Small Business Management course at the local community college. I decided not to continue the class but forgot to drop the course. I simply walked away. I unknowingly acquired an 'E' on my transcript instead of what would have been an 'I' for Incomplete.

I took time to go back to graduate school in order to try to reboot myself. I chose a historically Black college to take my graduate level Education courses. Bowie state to be exact. I learned a lot but unfortunately the only class I really enjoyed was the class where the professor was White. But not before driving myself up to Columbia University to speak directly with an advisor about the Master of Journalism program. Although I never became a Broadcast Journalist, *Vantage Point* makes me sort of glad that I didn't. At least not somewhere dealing with political conflict. An actor/actress using my name is being blown-up while reporting. Maybe I can write stories for a newspaper or magazine, from 'home', Lol. I am now writing. I hope to write a few articles and books.

It's 1976 and I am 3 years old. The name of the Steakhouse has changed and our mother's were very close before mine passed away a little over 10 years ago. My middle name is her first name and our profiles are similar. I pray that neither one of our ships are sinking as on April 14, 1912. Although I'm the single parent, that's her mother's name. Her daughter is the one who is hard to impress in the movie Titanic. Is it September 11, 1792? Well, I'm not married. I hope she is.

I'm not feeling very lucky anymore, but I know I'm blessed.

Until We Meet Again

(You can build a castle but you just can't live in it. (My brother the Day Laborer). You're the fastest runner but you're not allowed to win. Doctor says you're cured, but you still feel the pain. (Can't find my mom's cancer because it's behind her stomach). Aspirations in the clouds but your hopes go down the drain. (Me; educated without a job)}.
I feel a world of prosecution against me. I am not the evil, whore-like, (can't take you home to momma), kind of woman that everyone thinks and expresses about me. In the movie, Why Did I Get Married, the guys are bashing some woman named Angela like she is a spawn of Satan.
I know I'm not loud and obnoxious so I wonder what they could possibly mean. I refuse to believe that straight men would actually admit out loud and/or go on television and say that a woman is bad at sex. That couldn't be what they mean. If I were a man in a relationship with a woman whom I knew very well, and she was naked, in my presence and I knew she loved me the way I loved her; I would let her know that I'm a manly man. I would sit down, put her on my lap, slide my penis in her vagina, put her titty in my mouth, grab her butt with both hands, and bounce gently; then I would marry her.

A past boyfriend shared with me that he had gone on a ski trip and met three other men who had slept with me. It was a bus trip. I've been on several ski trips; all as a youngster. I've never had sex on any of them. So to the four guys who didn't even know each other before the ski trip, where they first met; you were obviously all sent there just to meet each other; just to sit in a circle and bash me; (you know who you are). (Four relationships that I'd had over an eight year period several years before I became homeless). You're bad at intimacy and relationships, not me! I'm a woman. I may not have smelled like roses, but I didn't smell bad. I'm not supposed to think to dominate you during intimacy. Especially if it's our first time having sex. I don't care if you thought you were too small to be on top. Then sit on the side of the bed and take my hand. And if your argument is that I was already lying down, then, that's called foreplay. Roll over and say ride me. It's a confidence that you all just didn't have. You were too worried about having sex with me so that you could call me a ho. And yes, you can have foreplay and not have sex. I believed you loved me; marriage was a given. You win; you happy? The entire world believes I'm a ho. Because I believed you felt the same, I'm unable to work.

You can say that I wasn't confident enough to sit on two people's penises, (in two serious relationships that have already been mentioned, where he was big enough to not need it), instead of sucking them but I can't believe you can't figure out on your own; why that happened. Not because I was pressed for a man or because I needed money or shelter. (I'm homeless and I'm a 'mute'; not mixed, just forbidden to speak, not literally; just figuratively because of the 'one friend at a time rule'). Yes literally! Who do I talk to if he works all day, every day! I am not pressed and I wasn't pressed then. It's never casual to me. I'm not a ho. I sat down on the man I love but my tiny breast weren't facing him. 'Oh yeah'; I'm just bad at sex. In my mind, if you haven't made an attempt to touch my breast in the bed, on the sofa, in the car or stopping me as I walk across the bedroom, why would I think you would touch them in the chair? You were hurting my feelings on purpose. So I'm shunned because I sat down backward? No one's ever taken control in the sitting position. I'm very happy single. For the rest of my life; trust me. Anyway; next topic.

How about the topic of women who go to Florida or New Orleans for Spring Break and sleep with more than one complete stranger while they are there. They return to become professors, consultants, archeologists, accountants, and landscapers. No one cares that they barred their breast and have beads hanging in their bedroom to show for it.

We can talk about *The Ugly Truth* if you'd like. The movie is definitely not about me. Although I did intern with a popular, black owned, radio station and at an advertising agency before I graduated. I remember sharing an elevator with the station owner once; she was nice. I'm assuming her and all of her cohorts love *The Devil Wears Prada* and the new show, being Mary Jane. Unfortunately, there not ugly. I wonder if they like the movie The Best Man.

Besides the one man I'm allowed to be friends with; no one talks to me. For years it's been this way. No one touches me. And neither my daughter nor my father, hug. I guess now for the rest of my life that man will be, my grandson. I guess I'll just talk to him until he's able to talk. I haven't had sex in a little over a year now. Ever since he's been born. (This is not a challenge for me, and never has been). Now I have someone to touch and someone to talk to. I can't stay here any longer without income and I can't take him with me to work. I pray that my books sell.

But, if I make a purpose to just document all of the things that I do to remind me that I'm alive, that aren't sex; with men, women, children, family members, complete strangers and by myself; It has not been that eventful of a year:

No plans for New Years. No plans for Valentine's Day. I dance around the apartment and outside. I smile a lot. I laugh. I hug people who want to be hugged when it's appropriate. I say good morning and thank you to my bus driver. I quit my part-time job due to verbal harassment from management. Full-time pan-handler again. My first grandchild was born. I became a free babysitter. I kissed my man (of four years); I let him suck on my titty's and stick his finger in my vagina. I broke up with him for good. My family; (my father, my daughter, my grandson and my daughter's boyfriend); took me to dinner for my birthday, to a place I'd already been. My daughter graduated from high school. We took my daughter out to dinner after her graduation. I saw her off to her prom. My daughter was hired as a cashier. My daughter found a job in the government. She's working both jobs. My daughter started college. I No longer have my beat up, used truck. But I still have this completely fabricated parking ticket. Now, how will I ever get my finances straight if the sabotage never stops? I've been given a $500 ticket that has now risen to $600. It was issued in Washington DC. So if I'm unable to get this money by pan-handling, I won't be able to drive. This is an opportunity for my race and Christian folk to come forth and purchase my book in support.

Anyway, what was I saying; oh yeah:

My daughter bought her first used car. We took my daughter to dinner for her birthday. Got my first mammogram. (Having a pronounced lump in my breast, can't be normal). I went to visit my mother's grave. We ordered carry out to eat at the hotel, for my father's birthday when he came into town. My daughter moved into her first apartment. My daughter broke up with her boyfriend, I think. I celebrated Thanksgiving with my extended and immediate family. My grandson had his first Christmas in his home, (my daughter's first apartment). No plans for New Year's. No plans for Valentine's Day. Had a big first birthday party for my grandson, and had a brief conversation on Facebook with my best girlfriend from elementary school; can you believe it; somebody talked to me. She even promised to bring her grandson to my grandson's birthday party. (She didn't show up). I spoke with her the other day and she is getting married really soon. I look forward to celebrating that day with her.

Hooray. My daughter just bought her first brand new car, all by herself. I'm so proud of her. Praise god, she no longer has that used car that can't pass inspection.

After all of this; I would have thought that attorneys would be chasing me. They obviously believe the lies too. When I received the money from my mother's death, they cut my hours. It wasn't that much to begin with. Do you understand what I'm saying? All of the children were literally acting like baboons so that none of the teachers would request me as their substitute. The S.I.M.S system couldn't help if the teacher didn't want you as their substitute. When you work all day, it's hard to find time to write a book or file a lawsuit without an attorney that you can't afford. It's also hard to find time and energy to go to the movies. When you work hard all day, you get home and you just want to stay there. Even when you're homeless; after a full day of pan-handling, you're tired. Entertaining company is great but going out and partying at night is not likely. (Can't have female company if no females ever talk to you.) The libel and slander that causes defamation, has always bothered me. And has always been successful at keeping me from maintaining friends and prospering. **Heavenly father; I refused the white man's invitation to move to a bordering county, only to be used by a few ignorant black people when I needed shelter after losing my job in the school-system; (No it was not casual to me). This book wasn't written to give excuses for why I had sex while I was homeless. No, I wasn't just doing what I had to, to survive. I think a part of me just wanted to see if someone could really be that evil. Wow; after all black people had been through. It truly makes me not want to vote for anyone Black, ever again. I am not a ho. I don't have sex so I can enjoy the feeling of cumming. And I do not sleep with people for employment, money or shelter.**

As a classroom of my students chanted one day; during a conversation about "my" sex-life; that they held amongst themselves as if it was part of the curriculum; "Nobody had a gun to her head." Assuming that everything they've seen is about me. But I know, I wasn't ho-ing. Because I don't even know what ho-ing is. Seven years. One teacher boyfriend whom I dated and became intimate with; in the entire school system. He invited me to fly with him to Europe, but I don't fly any longer; I'm claustrophobic. (I know I need to stop confessing that.) I guess your attempt to get me out of the country didn't work.

Here is where I attempt to begin a writing career. I'm quite sure you're having a focus group on how to sabotage this. It's almost flattering.

Trying to replace public shame with 'something else', is not the same as telling the truth after you've been lied on for 20 to 30 years to protect someone else's feelings. When your spouse watches *Bridesmaids* and sees me riding the male actor instead of you, in the back of his mind; that's a problem. That's not normal.

I mean think about it. I traveled to and returned from Europe, a virgin at age 15. The only movie that I know of, that really focuses on a young female virgin that age 15, is the one where a 15 year old virgin goes to Europe, gets kidnapped and is used as a sex slave. *Taken.* Maybe I was cast and stuck in the movie Django.

Let me just say this. When I was in elementary school, there was a girl who smelled really bad, every day. No one wanted to sit next to her. I'm quite sure she didn't have a boyfriend. Even though I'm sure the teacher already knew, we finally told the teacher so that the teacher could let her know. We didn't tease her. We weren't mean to her.

The way I smell is not provable. Because people lie. Now supposedly, in a small house, in an area where there are three tables with at least 25-30 dishes of food; on Thanksgiving, I smell bad. I entered the house not smelling. The point is supposed to be that I need to change my pad more frequently. Now afterward, I rode with my father in his pickup truck. I didn't smell anything. But supposedly, he did. I know if I smell fishy and I know if I smell like urine. I'm not saying this because it hurts for people to tell me I smell. They are all being ridiculous. I'm not crying because the truth hurts. I'm crying because everyone believes the lies and others continue to tell more lies.

Please remember; Conditioning is science. Science is exact and provable. However, it becomes a weird science when you use it in the wrong way.

My hair is healthy because I care for it. My teeth are healthy because I care for them. My skin is clear because I care for it; also because I have regular bowel movements. I'm at peace when I'm alone because my spirit is full of real love, always. After an unprofessional person infected my toenail, I tended to it regularly and it's getting better. Why would I not pay attention to the way my underarms or vagina smell?

If I've always worn a pad that I don't change regularly enough and I consequently smell, how was I able to meet all of these men to even talk and hang out and sometimes kiss, for the past 30 years? The women are now attempting to answer this question as I walk around and pan handle. Either they're not very smart or it makes them feel better about themselves to believe and say to me that they "don't have any change right now but they may or they will when they come out", (of the grocery store). Implying that I'm single because I smell after sex. There's a lot of other reasons to not be able to get or keep a man, when you're unemployed and homeless. But if the entire population believes your hygiene is bad, you will probably be unemployed and homeless forever. That's their goal remember, to keep me in loser status.

All of the movies are not an exact truth about me. (I'm not you and you're not me). Pay attention to each movie you watch and understand the message that is meant for you. And if it's not exactly true, it's exactly false…..Yeah, there's Hertz and there's not exactly. Just because it hurts; that doesn't mean it's true. That has nothing to do with the things that your children see on TV and use as fuel to harass his or her teacher, as you sit by and condone it. I've made mistakes. Let it go.

(You may think I'm crazy, and you are entitled to your opinion. Just please don't harass me with your opinion.)

Now say, "All this, and now she's writing this because she's hurt"? As if going on a shooting rampage would have been the better choice when I first saw the group of movies attempting to sabotage me. So which response do you want? Now try to sue me for my money if I earn any from the book that exposes the breach of my civil rights. What response do you think you'll get from that? Prayerfully; divine intervention. Not the reaction the actor/actress gave in "Why Did I Get Married."

My heart is broken because my cousins and former girlfriends don't want to go out or invite me to their homes. My heart is broken because my daughter never had a dating relationship with her college educated, Christian father. My heart is broken at the thought that I will never have a best friend or life-mate. My heart is broken because I should never be interrogated by anyone about why I had sex with a few men whom I loved in different ways than typical, and will never forget, during this hurtful, **forced** homeless situation that has not yet ended. But my soul is completely gutted and left hollow at the thought that every black person on this planet exhales with satisfaction in knowing that my life's story has been mangled and thrown about like a train wreck; even before I made the mistake of believing that men wanted sexual spontaneity in a relationship.

What I thought was a great way to get to know someone before you become intimate, was completely ignored during the process of harassing me. A typical date is dinner and a movie, I guess. When I was invited to live with my ex-boyfriends sister after being left outside; we all drove home together and then played board games until mid-nite; for about a month. I made it clear then, that I didn't want to play house and that I wasn't a ho. You can learn a lot about someone by playing Taboo or Scattergories. He would visit me during his lunch–time if I wasn't already busy pan-handling. There were a lot of other reasons why the relationship ended and I do not believe I was at fault. I am not a cheater. I did not cheat on him. I was put in the role of a homeless woman who was lied to by her boyfriend. That doesn't make me a ho. The majority of the time I live in the hotel I paid for. And the men I stayed with did not come on to me or pretend to make me a girlfriend. Yeah a few men lead me on but I wasn't ho-ing. Don't get it twisted.

The men from past relationships, prior to me being homeless, can lie and say that the reason why our relationship didn't work out is because I smelled but that is an enormous lie. I remember the first time I smelled after intimacy. It was after I became homeless. Very rare. Only a few times and it was because I'd had a miscarriage from a previous pregnancy in a previous relationship. I didn't look pregnant. I was pudgy but wearing two winter coats to stay worn can create a really fat torso. (I had gotten pregnant by my 7 year on and off relationship partner). And no I don't need to refresh more, I need to enjoy my life more.

Is there one decent person who is able to assist me in my attempt to earn a living and keep a roof over my head, without a male life-mate and without sleeping on my daughter's sofa? Working a nine to five, is not an option. Writing for a newspaper or magazine from home is an option. Doing hair in the basement of my home is also an option.

I have a lump in my breast and I have no health insurance. I'm paying monthly to my Insurance carrier just to get a yearly check-up. I'm supposed to pay for everything else. I have no money. It's murder. I do not now, nor have I ever intentionally cheated with the intent of deceiving my mate. I have never intentionally tried to break-up someone else's marriage. I would never intentionally share a man. I would never intentionally be a ho. Please help me. I don't need you to predict what I'm going to say or do and then say I'm repeating you. I need you to help me get through the sabotage of having no income, etc. I am not obeying commands, although I have been conditioned to a certain extent. I remember my mother saying, "If I listen to the doctors, I'd just be sitting around crying all day." I guess that's why she continued working and tried to stick to her usual routine. Well, I just watched the movie called A Joyful Noise and if I sit and watch movies and listen to secular or gospel music all day, I'd probably sit around crying all day too. The information that is being twisted and misleading to viewers. Oh my God. It's overwhelming.

You called yourselves getting me back when I didn't know enough math to teach. You stuck my daughter in classrooms with long-term substitutes who didn't lecture or give out homework. You did that to my daughter because you thought I was a prostitute. I went to graduate school for a refresher course and to prepare myself for the classroom.

This is a shout out to all department heads in every school on every level. Meet with your long–term substitutes to go over what is being taught and the progress of the academic goals on a weekly basis. Don't make them have to try to hunt you down.

To all the single ladies, whether you've been married or not; knowing that it is your desire to be married, I would never say to you, you are single because you smell or because you are just a ho. I can confidently say that; knowing that anyone who is reading this, 270 page book, is not retarded.

For those of you who are a little slow or love challenged; let me break it down for you. I'm not more in love with any man right now, over another; I do not have a man. Each asshole had a chance to convince me that he was worthy of my love. I believe that God wanted me to be with the man who took vows with me or the man with whom I lost my virginity, if I choose to be with a man at all. My heart was always been open for love and marriage but I'm happy single. Lord forgive me for cursing. I want to be used by God. I truly want to enjoy the company of a friend. Male or female.

I've never had sex with two people at once but even if I decided to have sex with three people at once, it's none of your business. I may not be an angel in your eyes but I'm not an un-repented sinner.

There's the voice of men saying it's too late to say all of this, you should just wait longer in your relationships with men. That didn't work either. I did not necessarily need to list the men I did not sleep with to try to prove that I'm not a ho.

Let me guess. After publishing the truth in this book, I won't be hired by those who violated my rights in the first place? (Don't be ridiculous. You never had a chance to be hired by such large companies in the first place.) Even though they made movies like Juwanna Mann that have the main character in my jersey number, on a female basketball team. I'm not an exhibitionist. I'm not conceited or rude. And I've never made out with any basketball team-mates. **The office scene they show, up against the desk; that is identical to that in the movie Hitch; is not true.** Juwanna's hair, as a man, is strikingly similar to how mine was cut and styled after my divorce. His female co-stars hair is like mine in my actual basketball picture. Her movie boyfriend is the real-life cousin of my ex from high school whom I met up with after my divorce. He was the one who'd just purchased the new Cadillac. I've just seen the movie for the first time, May 2015. Yes Disney, for some reason, I've lost all of my friends. Earlier when I spoke of being shunned, I still hadn't seen the movie yet. Attorneys chase ambulances. Why didn't they come find me? Oh, they sent a Black female attorney to come and get a bikini wax from me. That's not why I'm single. Clearly, everybody wants me to stay broke.

In *Diary of a Mad Black Woman*. That's my rich doctor; former friend's hand-me-down car from her dad. And 'my' favorite spot (restaurant) in the world; that's her name. (I'm not saying this to be disrespectful).

Yeah Disney, it's "Girl Meets World". I guess it's hard to take on the world when the entire world is misled!

Our (20 year) neighbors to the right share the last name of the capital of Texas. The youngest son married a stripper. He was warned to be careful by the 'Knight' in *Pretty Woman*. He's the spitting image of the dark-skinned guy with the locks from *The Best Man*. Before their father died last year, he told me I was invited to live with all of them in N.C.. He still lived here and he knew I was homeless. Had I moved in with them, she would have known that she was his dream, because I would have been there.

Ok so I'm sleeping on my daughter's sofa. I know the saying, beggars can't be choosy. But can I have my life back please? I'm getting messages from those around me, I suppose from those who've violated my rights, that it's too late to sue them or tell the truth. So I suppose if no one purchases my book, I will just be homeless forever.

I've been given an ultimatum by planet Earth. Either I can befriend drug-dealing, whore-minded, uneducated folks or I can sit and stare at the wall for eternity. I think I'd better go get my mother's beautiful artwork and hang it up. Not because they think I sold sex but because they believe I had sex too easily with too many people.

Had I married the thick, dark-skinned Black guy in Brown Sugar, who was singing "The ho is mine", my name would have been: The Keys In '**A. Minor**'. Are you familiar with the album? She's never met me or even held a conversation with me; but this album made her a millionaire.

No *'Love Doesn't Cost a thing'* and yes I had my first car accident in front of **Morgan** State University while in college. My father told me that my car sustained **$3,000** worth of damage. He was the one who changed my brakes, my oil, and showed me how to change a flat tire after I'd gotten stranded and couldn't change it myself. My mother passed away a few months before this movie was released. I suppose they care about my father and did not want him to have unprotected sex. Or were they mocking the fact that I bought a box of condoms before I visited California for the first time. Did not have sex when I got there; but I had condoms. I never buy condoms. (And no I was not expecting to have sex). I'm sure I could have found someone if that were my desire. Bottom line; I didn't pay anyone and no one paid me, for sex; ever.

I can't walk past stationary Jehovah's witnesses at the subway station without hearing; "Oh now you're a ho". (…from the woman) and, "Well what was it then?"(…from the man). (It is May 2015) Everyone thinks I smell. Excuse me; smelled in every relationship I've had. They believe that the plane crashes and train derailments are because I know people and I'm hurt because no one wants me. I can't sit on the metro bus without the person behind me saying out loud; "Cause you're a ho."

My first book is a poetry book and I would like to deliver copies that I've finally had completed, to churches; and I would like to go to certain people's homes to ask for a purchase of support. My daughter told me to take her car yesterday to pan-handle all day but she will not allow me to drop her at work and keep her car tomorrow so that I can sell my poetry book. Is it me or does it seem like I'm being held against my will to keep me poor? It is now a consensus among all humans that I am unfit to be in a healthy, monogamous relationship. No man is interested. It is May 2015. I am to come to grips with 'never having hope' for finding my very own man.

I just saw the movie *Hope Floats* for the first time (May 2015). This movie came out in 1998, when I was newly divorced and sometimes hosting male company in my apartment. I'm being indirectly told as I watch this movie that everyone knew then, that the actor/actress was portraying me. See I had a little girl and I was single. They believe that I needed to wash up before intimacy, as portrayed by the actor/actress. Then many years later I'm allegedly sitting on the counter in my apartment, alone, asking why no one wants me; as shown in *Miss Congeniality* by the same actor/actress. It doesn't bother be that they are obsessed with me in Hollywood but I wish I knew that everyone believed all of these things about me before I attempted to develop a relationship with those men whom I welcomed into my life. (This is where the ignorant, childish, random comments of, "Well what was it then?", come from. No, I've never had sex in a white oxford shirt with no bottoms; *Hope floats* and *Notorios BIG*.

Could the showing of the movie *Hope Floats* last night and the fact that I can't tread water, but just flip and float on my back, be a sign that the young woman I met yesterday while pan-handling, who has her own indoor playground not far from here, will really be able to HELP me get my writing career going by assisting me in promoting my poetry book. I consider this Devine intervention and beneficial networking. When you see me cry, know that my tears are not falling for the reason you probably think. But I see that it gives you great joy to think I'm not happy and that you can cause great misery in my life; say what you will to make yourself look and feel better. If I were a ho I would say so. I have no one to answer to but God.

Read this book again. Pay attention. Believe and understand what you've read here, as you've believed that trash you've read previously by other authors. Then change your ways. I'm not a ho. It's you who needs to change. My conscience is clear and it always has been. Is yours?

Do you all really believe that finding the perfect man for me and/or, me not having to work (because I'm the designated sitter for my now toddler aged grandson), can heal the pains of an entire world stabbing me in my back? Although I have yet to receive that large wad of money, one may say, I'm no longer clueless. All of the clues that I've been given, have made me more aware. The significance of the letters **BP** and the movie **300**. Stop *Changing Lanes* so you won't *Crash*. The **black and white** bunny cartoon characters with the big breast and the woman with the big nose, who shares my middle name as her first; being the **base pair** because both have fathers whom were in the military. The other woman will have big breast and I have an ugly nose; so I will not win in a competition for a man. Am I warm yet or am I getting colder? From what I've read, it appears that this **horrible disease; (HIV)** can live in ones system for a long time. I praise God that I don't have it. And I purpose in my heart to find a way to remember every day, those who died from it and those who are still living with it. I Love You and May God Continue to Bless You.

My mother's legacy was her hospitality. She took pictures of everyone and kept those pictures that were given to her. No matter how many years went by. My father and the rest of my family seem to think that throwing all of this stuff in the trash is a good way to make me cry. They don't see that they are throwing my mother's legacy away. The awards that she got for being a dedicated team mother, were what made her the happiest. Why would my father want to throw that stuff away. We are about to be thrown out of our apartment and may possibly lose our storage. I took the pictures and trophies from the storage and brought them into the apartment. Now what?

Now that everyone thinks that Diary of a Mad Black Woman is about me or my former friend Chandra; because it's her car. My ex-boyfriend Brian, looks just like that guy in the movie, with braids and everything and his wife "ex" wife, looks just like the woman. I never saw myself in that role because I've never been riding in a vehicle with any guy, talking mean and sounding bitter like that. (He always did keep baby-oil in his apartment. I thought he was actually divorced). Let me stop speculating.

Shallow Hal: I'm the girl who got good grades and is not scared to be funny. I had lots of friends who were boys who evidentally never thought of themselves as my boyfriend when they actually were. Every writer is calling me a ho and those actors playing me have a role that states I'm ugly. She's wearing my shirt, driving Aunt Florrie and Bianca's car and using my cousin, Gwen's name.

The information you are about to read is just a small reason why my brother and I should never spend a day in jail for pan-handling or, not paying a traffic ticket that wasn't real to begin with. And we should not have to run for our lives either:

My brother's name is Carlos Jerome Williams. My father is Jerry Williams. He is 73 years old and he was born on September 22. Our close family friend is Linda Person; an attorney. My daughter's name is Indigo Skye; "Hi, Blue". We blamed it all on you. Well not you, but, your mother and you. (Rio).

Jerome Leon Bruckheimer or "Jerry"Bruckheimer; born September 21, 1943; age 70. Spouse; Linda. Movies: Without a trace; Soldier of Fortune, Inc; E-Ring; Max Q; and Bad Boys. Just to name a few.

The entire world is stealing my book as I write it. They refuse to buy it, even for $5 or $6 bucks. They all think that immediate family is crazy. And our offspring. It'sabotage! My father raised his children. We both have high school diplomas. He's a Marine and I'm educated through one year of graduate school (and I have a trade license). Then the talk show hosts say, you were the only one in your family who cared about your brother because he was homeless for a little while. Now you're the only one who cares about your daughter. But they're all married and I'm not. Man if I had big titties. Now there's the Smarter Sentencing Act up for a vote. I understand that 50% of inmates don't have high school diplomas. But you harass me off of my substitute teaching job and now I'm homeless because of it. My daughter has her diploma and she can read. I'm pushing her to get a college degree. She's already finished several classes.

I met 'April' yesterday at Mission of Love in Capitol Heights, MD while completing my community service hours for supposedly, 'trespassing'. She looks just like Gabrielle Union with much larger breast. Is it pieces of her or pieces of me?

As long as I only make pocket change selling my books, no one cares; but if I were to make enough to buy a car or house or God forbid I earn so much that I don't need to work any longer, then I will have problems with "slander" lawsuits against me? My book is not slandering anyone. Just wanted everyone aware of the slander against my daughter and myself. Please help me and my daughter.

www.ingramcontent.com/pod-product-compliance
Lightning Source LLC
Chambersburg PA
CBHW071237280526
45787CB00002B/970